G000255266

Great Irish Quotations

First published in 2009 by
Appletree Press Ltd
The Old Potato Station
14 Howard Street South
Belfast BT7 1AP

Tel: +44 (0) 28 90 24 30 74
Fax: +44 (0) 28 90 24 67 56
Email: reception@appletree.ie
Web: www.appletree.ie

Copyright © Appletree Press, 2009
Text compiled by Sean McMahon
Additional text compiled by Jean Brown
Photographs as acknowledged on page 96

First published by Appletree Press in 1994 as *A Little Book of Irish Quotations*

All rights reserved. Printed in China. No part of this publication may be reproduced or transmitted, in any form or by any means, electronic or mechanical, photocopying, recording, or in any information and retrieval system, without permission in writing from the copyright owner.

A catalogue record for this book is available from the British Library.

Great Irish Quotations

ISBN: 978 1 84758 119 8

Desk & Marketing Editor: Jean Brown
Copy-editing: Jim Black
Designer: Stuart Wilkinson
Production Manager: Paul McAvoy

9 8 7 6 5 4 3 2 1

AP3601

Great Irish Quotations

Sean McMahon

Contents

Jonathan Swift

Out of Ireland Have I Come

This [the Irish] is a filthy people, wallowing in vice. Of all peoples it is the least instructed in the rudiments of the faith.

Giraldus Cambrensis *c. 1147-c. 1223*
Topographica Hiberniae

She is of a gentle nature. If the anger of heaven be against her she will not bluster or storme, but she will weep many days together.

Justice Luke Gerson *fl. 1620*
Ireland Delineated

Fair LIBERTY was all his cry.

Jonathan Swift *1667-1745*
Verses on the Death of Dr Swift

He gave the little wealth he had
To found a house for fools and mad:
And show'd by one satiric touch,
No nation wanted it so much.

Jonathan Swift
Verses on the Death of Dr Swift

Amazed the gazing rustics rang'd around,
And still they gaz'd and still the wonder grew,
That one small head could carry all he knew.

Oliver Goldsmith *1730-74*
The Deserted Village

Whenever I wanted to know what the Irish people wanted, I had only to examine my own heart and it told me straight off what the Irish people wanted.

Eamon De Valera *1882-1975*
Dáil Éireann, 6 January 1922

In Ireland a policeman's lot is a supremely happy one. God smiles, the priest beams, and the novelist groans.

Sean Ó Faoláin *1900-92*
The Dilemma of Irish Letters

Ireland is a fruitful mother of genius, but a barren nurse.

John Boyle O'Reilly *1844-90*
Watchwords

Think where man's glory most begins and ends,
And say my glory was I had such friends.

W B Yeats *1865-1939*
The Municipal Gallery Revisited

Out of Ireland have we come,
Great hatred, little room,
Maimed us from the start.
I carry from my mother's womb
A fanatic heart.

W B Yeats
Remorse for Intemperate Speech

Then let the Orange Lily be
Thy badge my patriot brother –
The everlasting Green for me;
And – we for one another.

John de Jean Frazer *1809-52*
Song for July 12, 1843

Subtleman: And how do you intend to live?
Teague: By eating, dear joy, when I can get it; and
by sleeping when I can get none: 'tish the fashion of
Ireland.

George Farquhar *1677-1707*
The Twin Rivals

Isaac Butt

For the great Gaels of Ireland
Are the men that God made man,
For all their wars are merry
And all their songs are sad.

G K Chesterton *1874-1936*
Ballad of the White Horse

O Ireland, isn't it grand you look –
Like a bride in her rich adornin'?
And with all the pent-up love of my heart
I bid you the top of the mornin'!

John Locke *1847-89*
The Exile's Return

And Ireland long a province be
A Nation once again!

Thomas Davis *1814-45*
A Nation Once Again

I have been accustomed to understand by Ireland, not merely a country possessing certain geographical features but a country inhabited by a certain people whom I know.

Isaac Butt *1813-79*
The Irish People and the Irish Land

In Ireland the inevitable never happens and the unexpected constantly occurs.

Sir John Pentland Mahaffy *1839-1919*

Come back again – Come back to us, sometime – won't you? Oh the heart-cry of the Gael! It is heard so often in Eirinn that the very echoes of the land have learned it.

William Bulfin *1864-1910*
Rambles in Eirinn

Ireland is a small but insuppressible island half an hour nearer the sunset than Great Britain.

Thomas Kettle *1880-1916*
On Crossing the Irish Sea

Irishness is not primarily a question of birth or blood or language; it is the condition of being involved in the Irish situation, and usually of being mauled by it.

Conor Cruise O'Brien *b. 1917*
Irishness

What I especially like about Englishmen is that after they have called you a thief and a liar and patted you on the back for being so charming in spite of it, they look honestly depressed if you fail to see that they are paying you a handsome compliment.

Robert Lynd *1879-1949*
Irish and English

This lovely land that always sent
Her writers and artists to banishment
And in the spirit of Irish fun
Betrayed her own leaders, one by one.

James Joyce *1882-1941*
Gas from a Burner

I will not serve that in which I no longer believe, whether it call itself my home, my fatherland, or my church: and I will try to express myself in some mode of life or art as freely as I can and as wholly as I can, using for my defence the *only* arms I allow myself to use – silence, exile and cunning.

James Joyce
A Portrait of the Artist as a Young Man

Thomas Moore

Do you know what Ireland is? asked Stephen with cold venom. Ireland is the old sow that eats her farrow.

James Joyce
A Portrait of the Artist as a Young Man

Erin, the tear and the smile in thine eyes
Blend like the rainbow that hangs in thy skies.

Thomas Moore *1779-1852*
Erin the Tear

Rich and rare were the gems she wore,
And a bright gold ring on her wand she bore;
But oh! her beauty was far beyond
Her sparkling gems and snow-white wand.

Thomas Moore
Rich and Rare

The harp that once thro' Tara's halls,
The soul of Music shed,
Now hangs as mute on Tara's walls
As if that soul were fled.

Thomas Moore
The Harp That Once

John Philpot Curran

...mad Ireland hurt you into poetry.
Now Ireland has her madness and her weather still,
For poetry makes nothing happen.

W H Auden *1907-1973*
In Memory of WB Yeats

Ireland's a door where the living collogue with the dead.

Francis MacManus *1909-65*
Praise God for Ireland

Dear Erin, how sweetly thy green bosom rises!
An emerald set in the ring of the sea.

John Philpot Curran *1750-1817*
Cushla Ma Chree

Laurence Sterne

The Humour Is On Me

Being moderately taken...it sloweth age, it strengtheneth youth, it helpeth digestion, it cutteth flegme, it abandoneth melancholie, it relisheth the heart, it lighteneth the mind, it quickeneth the spirits...

Richard Stanihurst *1547-1618*
Aqua Vitae

I wish either my father or mother, or indeed both of them, as they were in duty both equally bound to it, had minded what they were about when they begot me.

Laurence Sterne *1713-68*
Tristram Shandy

Brian O'Linn and his wife and wife's mother,
They all crossed over the bridge together.
The bridge broke down and they all tumbled in –
'We'll go home by water', said Brian O'Linn.

Anonymous *18th Century*
Brian O'Linn

A circulating library in a town is an ever-green tree of diabolical knowledge! It blossoms through the year!

Richard Brinsley Sheridan *1759-1816*
The Rivals

You've heard o' Julius Caesar
an' the great Napoleon too,
And how the Cork Militia bate the Turks at Waterloo
But there's a page of history that,
as yet, remains uncut:
An' that's the Martial story
o' the Shlathery's Mounted Fut.

Percy French *1854-1920*
Slattery's Mounted Fut

On Egypt's banks, contagious to the Nile
The auld Pharaoh's daughter,
She went to bathe in style.
She took her dip and she came unto the land
And to dry her royal pelt she ran along the strand.

Zozimus *1794-1846*
The Finding of Moses

O long life to the man who invinted potheen –
Sure the Pope ought to make him a martyr –
If myself was this moment Victoria, our Queen,
I'd drink nothing but whiskey and wather.

Zozimus
In Praise of Potheen

Saint Patrick was a gintleman,
He came of decent people,
In Dublin town he built a church,
And upon't put a steeple;
His father was an O'Callaghan,
His mother was a Brady,
His aunt was an O'Shaughnessy,
His uncle was a Grady.

Zozimus
Saint Patrick Was a Gintleman

Anyone acquainted with Ireland knows that the morning of St Patrick's Day consists of the night of the 17th of March, flavoured strongly with the morning of the 18th.

'Ballyhooley' (Robert J Martin)
St Patrick's Day in the Morning

It's only a little cold I have; there's nothing derogatory wrong with me.

Sean O'Casey
The Plough and the Stars

All I ever seemed to get was the kind of girl who had a special dispensation from Rome to wear the thickest part of her legs below the knee.
Hugh Leonard *b.1926*
Da

My grandmother made dying her life's work.

Hugh Leonard
Home before Night

'More rain coming,' said Mr Knox, rising composedly; 'you'll have to put a goose down these chimneys some day soon, it's the only way to clean them.'

Somerville & Ross (Edith Oenone Somerville *1858-1949* **and Violet Martin** *1862-1915*)
Some Experiences of an Irish RM

Here's to the Pope in Killybuck, and may there be strife between Orange and Green as long as Alexander McCracken has a bad farm of land to sell.

Louis J Walsh *1880-1942*
The Pope in Killybuck

When money's tight and is hard to get
And your horse has also ran,
When all you have is a heap of debt –
A PINT OF PLAIN IS YOUR ONLY MAN.

Flann O'Brien *1911-66*
At Swim-Two-Birds

The gross and net result of it is that people who spend
most of their natural lives riding iron bicycles over the
rocky roadsteads of this parish get their personalities
mixed up with the personalities of their bicycles as
a result of the interchanges of the atoms of each of
them and you would be surprised at the number of
people in these parts who are nearly half people and
half bicycles.

Flann O'Brien
The Third Policeman

An' as it blowed an' blowed, I often looked up at the
sky an' assed meself the question – what is the stars,
what is the stars?

Sean O'Casey *1880-1964*
Juno and the Paycock

She's as headstrong as an allegory
on the banks of the Nile.

Richard Brinsley Sheridan *1759-1816*
The Rivals

Sir:
I am not so great a fool as you take me for. I have
been bitten once by you, and I will never give you an
opportunity of taking two bites of
A. Cherry

Andrew Cherry *1762-1812*
Letter to the manager of a Dublin theatre

In Glendalough lived a young saint,
In odour of sanctity dwelling,
An old-fashioned odour, which now
We seldom or never are smelling.

Samuel Lover *1797-1868*
St Kevin

Of priests we can offer a charming variety,
Far renowned for larnin' and piety;
Still I'd advance ye widout impropriety,
Father O'Flynn as the flower of them all.

A P Graves *1846-1931*
Father O'Flynn

Samuel Lover

Richard Brinsley Sheridan

My Love and I Did Meet

Here's to the maiden of bashful fifteen;
Here's to the widow of fifty;
Here's to the flaunting extravagant quean;
And here's to the housewife that's thrifty.

Richard Brinsley Sheridan *1759-1816*
The School for Scandal

Oh! hast thou forgotten this day we must part?
It may be for years and it may be for ever.

Julia Crawford *c.1799-c.1860*
Kathleen Mavourneen

I'm very lonely now, Mary,
For the poor make no new friends.

Lady Helen Selina Sheridan Blackwood Dufferin
1807-1867
Lament of the Irish Emigrant

But the heart that has truly loved, never forgets,
But as truly loves on to the close.

Thomas Moore *1779-1852*
Believe Me

…there's nothing half so sweet in life
As love's young dream.'

Thomas Moore
Oh, The Days Are Gone

My only books
Were Woman's looks,
And Folly's all they taught me.

Thomas Moore
The Time I've lost

She is far from the land where her young hero
    sleeps,
And lovers around her are sighing;
But coldly she turns from their gaze, and weeps
For her heart in his grave is lying.

Thomas Moore
She is Far from the Land

Well, the heart's a wonder; and, I'm thinking, there
won't be our like in Mayo, for gallant lovers, from this
hour today.

J M Synge *1871-1909*
The Playboy of the Western World

Oh, I'd rather live in poverty with little Mary Cassidy
Than Emperor without her be o'er Germany or Spain.

Francis Arthur Fahy *1854-1935*
Little Mary Cassidy

When you are old and grey and full of sleep,
And nodding by the fire, take down this book,
And slowly read, and dream of the soft look
Your eyes had once and of their shadows deep.

W B Yeats *1865-1939*
When You Are Old

Edmund Burke

On the Edge

She lays it on with a trowel.

William Congreve *1670-1729*
The Double Dealer

Alack, he's gone the way of all flesh.

William Congreve
Squire Bickerstaff Detected

The Irish are a fair people; – they never speak well of one another.

Samuel Johnson *1709-84*
Boswell, *Life of Johnson*

It is the nature of all greatness not to be exact.

Edmund Burke *1729-97*
American Taxation

Too nice an inquisition should not be made into opinions that are dying away by themselves.

Edmund Burke
Letter to Samuel Span

You should always except the present company.

John O'Keefe *1747-1833*
The London Hermit

Happiness is no laughing matter.
Richard Whately, Archbishop of Dublin *1787-1863*
Apophthegms

She's the sort of woman who lives for others – you can always tell the others by their hunted expression.

C S Lewis *1898-1963*
The Screwtape Letters

I have just read a long novel by Henry James. Much of it made me think of the priest condemned for a long space to confess nuns.

John Butler Yeats *1839-1922*

It [the Turko-Grecian war, 1912-13] was like waiting for a train in Mullingar.

Stephen MacKenna *1872-1934*

In those days the common people ideally separated the gentry of the country into three classes according to the relative degree of respect to which they considered it was entitled. They generally divided them thus: 1 Half-mounted gentlemen; 2 Gentlemen every inch of them; 3 Gentlemen to the backbone.

Sir Jonah Barrington *1760-1834*
Personal Sketches

Last week I saw a woman flayed, and you will hardly believe how much it altered her person for the worse.

Jonathan Swift *1667-1745*
Digression on Madness

The Carmelites will do their best to get him. He would be wasted with them – the boy ought to be a scholar, not a pulpit wind-bag.

Jeremiah 'Gerald' O'Donovan *1871-1942*
Father Ralph

Peel's smile was like the silver plate on a coffin.
Daniel O'Connell *1775-1848*

From left: Oliver Goldsmith, James Boswell and Dr Samuel Johnson

As I Roved Out

In burgo Duno tumulo; tumulantur in uno
Brigida, Patricius, atque Columba Pius.

[In Down three saints one grave do fill
Brigid, Patrick and Colmcille.]

John de Courcy *d.1219*

Boswell: Is not the Giant's Causeway worth seeing?
Johnson: Worth seeing? Yes, but not worth going to
see.

Samuel Johnson *1709-84*
Boswell, *Life of Johnson*

O stony grey soil of Monaghan
The laugh from my love you thieved.

Patrick Kavanagh *1904-67*
Stony Grey Soil

The bar-room was forgotten and all that concerned
it, and the things he saw most clearly were the green
hillside, and the bog-lake and the rushes about it, and
the greater lake in the distance, and behind it the blue
line of wandering hills.

George Moore *1852-1933*
Home Sickness

Charles Lever

But – hark! – some voice like thunder spake:
The West's awake! The West's awake!

Thomas Davis *1814-1845*
Home Sickness

And this is the beautiful land of scenery; and this is
the climate; and this the amusing and witty peasant
we read of. I have half a mind to tell the world how it
has been humbugged!

Charles Lever *(1806-1872)*
Lord Kilgobbin

But if at those roses you ventured to sip
The colour might all come away on your lip
So I'll wait for the wild rose that's waitin' for me –
Where the Mountains of Mourne sweep down to
    the sea.

Percy French
The Mountains of Mourne

…my sentimental regard for Ireland does not include
the capital.

George Bernard Shaw *1856–1950*
Immaturity

Your first day in Dublin is always your worst.

John Berryman *1914–1972*
Home Sickness

Yes, the newspapers were right; snow was general all over Ireland. It was falling on every part of the dark central plain, on the treeless hills, falling softly upon the Bog of Allen and, farther westward, softly falling into the dark mutinous Shannon waves.

James Joyce *1882-1941*
The Dead

riverrun, past Eve and Adam's, from swerve of shore to bend of bay, brings us by a circuitous vicus of recirculation back to Howth Castle and Environs.

James Joyce
Finnegans Wake

'But in the lonely hush of eve
Weeping I grieve the silent bills.'
I heard the Poor Old Woman say
In Derry of the little hills.

Francis Ledwidge *1891-1917*
Lament for the Poets: 1916

Red brick in the suburbs, white horse on the wall,
Eyetalian marbles in the City Hall:
O stranger from England, why stand so aghast?
May the Lord in his mercy be kind to Belfast.

Maurice James Craig *b.1919*
Ballad to a Traditional Refrain

I take my stand by the Ulster names,
each clean hard name like a weathered stone;
Tyrella, Rostrevor, are flickering flames:
the names I mean are the Moy, Malone,
Strabane, Slieve Gullion and Portglenone.

John Hewitt *1907-87*
Ulster Names

In doggerel and stout let me honour this country
Though the air is so soft that it smudges the words.

Louis MacNeice *1907-63*
Western Landscape

Armagh: where two cathedrals sit upon opposing hills
like the horns of a dilemma.

Sam Hanna Bell *1909-90*
In Praise of Ulster

George Moore

Dear Thoughts

But with the actor it is different: we are born at the rise of the curtain and we die with its fall, and every night in the presence of our patrons we write our new creation, and every night it is blotted out forever; and of what use is it to say to audience or to critic, 'Ah but you should have seen me last Tuesday!'

Micheál mac Liammóir *1899-1978*
Hamlet in Elsinore

I shall not go to heaven when I die,
But if they will let me be
I think I'll take the road I use to know
That goes by Shere-na-garagh and the sea.

Helen Waddell *1889-1965*
I Shall not Go to Heaven

We are the music makers,
We are the dreamers of dreams.

Arthur O'Shaughnessy *1841-81*
Ode

There is a lake in every man's heart...and he listens to its monotonous whisper year by year until at last he ungirds.

George Moore *1852-1933*
The Lake

Och! but I'm weary of mist and dark,
And roads where there's never a house or bush!

Padraic Colum *1881-1957*
An Old Woman of the Roads

There is wishful thinking in Hell as well as on earth.

C S Lewis *1898-1963*
The Screwtape Letters

I remember on one occasion when she [his mother] was asked to sing the English version of that touching melody 'The Red-haired Man's Wife', she replied, 'I will sing it for you; but the English words and the air are like a quarrelling man and wife; the Irish melts into the tune but the English doesn't.'

William Carleton *1794-1869*
Traits and Stories of the Irish Peasantry

But the age of chivalry is gone. That of the sophisters, economists and calculators has succeeded.

Edmund Burke *1729-97*
Reflections on the Revolution in France

Men thought it a region of sunshine and rest,
And they called it Hy-Brasail, the isle of the blest.

Gerald Griffin *1803-49*
Hy-Brasail

Honesty is the best policy; but he that is governed by
that maxim is not an honest man.

Richard Whately, Archbishop of Dublin *1787-1863*
Apophthegms

Dear thoughts are in my mind
And my soul soars enchanted,
As I hear the sweet lark sing
In the clear air of the day.

Sir Samuel Ferguson *1810-86*
The Lark in the Clear Air

It was like a miracle; but before our very eyes, and
almost in the drawing of a breath, the whole body
crumbled into dust and passed from our sight.

Abraham ('Bram') Stoker *1847-1912*
Dracula

Oliver Goldsmith

When lovely woman stoops to folly
And finds too late that men betray,
What charm can soothe her melancholy,
What art can wash her guilt away?

Oliver Goldsmith *1730-74*
The Vicar of Wakefield

Satire is a sort of glass wherein beholders do generally discover everyone's face but their own.

Jonathan Swift *1667-1745*
The Battle of the Books

Instead of dirt and poison we have rather chosen to fill our hives with honey and wax; thus furnishing mankind with the two noblest of things, which are sweetness and light.

Jonathan Swift
The Battle of the Books

He had been eight years upon a project for extracting sunbeams out of cucumbers, which were to be put into phials hermetically sealed, and let out to warm the air in raw inclement summers.

Jonathan Swift
Gulliver's Travels

And he gave it for his opinion, that whoever could make two ears of corn or two blades of grass to grow upon a spot of ground where only one grew before, would deserve better of mankind, and do more essential service to his country than the whole race of politicians put together.

Jonathan Swift
Gulliver's Travels

The intellect is forced to choose
Perfection of the life, or of the work.

W B Yeats *1865-1939*
The Choice

I see His blood upon the rose
And in the stars the glory of His eyes.

Joseph Mary Plunkett *1887-1916*
I See His Blood upon the Rose

The beauty of the world hath made me sad,
This beauty that will pass.

Patrick Pearse *1879-1916*
The Wayfarer

W B Yeats

In a good play every speech should be as fully flavoured as a nut or apple.

J M Synge *1871-1909*
The Playboy of the Western World

Don't strike me. I killed my poor father, Tuesday was a week, for doing the like of that.

J M Synge
The Playboy of the Western World

It's the life of a young man to be going on the sea, and who would listen to an old woman with one thing and she saying it over.

J M Synge
Riders to the Sea

What! No music; no dancing at Castle Hermitage tonight; and all the ladies sitting in a formal circle; petrifying into perfect statues.

Maria Edgeworth *1768-1849*
Ormond

Home! A good place to be going on top o' the world. Home I would be going myself – but sure, the night is young and we are in no hurry.

Maurice Walsh *1879-1964*
The Quiet Man and Other Stories

Paddy Bawn and Ellen Roe were married. One small statement – and it holds the risk of tragedy, the probability of resigned acceptance, the chance of happiness: choices as wide as the world.

Maurice Walsh
The Quiet Man and Other Stories

You must remain at home while she is with us, entertain her while I am occupied, walk with her, dance with her, be her beau.

Gerald Griffin *1803-1840*
The Collegians

Oscar Wilde

The Importance of Being Oscar

Absinthe
After the first glass of absinthe you see things as you wish they were. After the second you see them as they are not. Finally you see things as they really are, and that is the most horrible thing in the world.

Said in conversation

Advice
I always pass on good advice. It is the only thing to do with it. It is never of use to oneself.

An Ideal Husband

Age
Thirty-five is a very attractive age. London society is full of women of the very highest birth who have, of their own free choice, remained thirty-five for years.

The Importance of Being Earnest

One should never trust a woman who tells one her real age. A woman who would tell one that would tell one anything.

A Woman of No Importance

No woman should ever be quite accurate about her age. It looks so calculating.

The Importance of Being Earnest

America and Americans
The youth of America is their oldest tradition. It has been going on now for three hundred years. To hear them talk one would imagine they were in their first childhood. As far as civilisation goes they are in their second.

A Woman of No Importance

All Americans lecture, I believe. I suppose it is something in their climate.

A Woman of No Importance

American girls are pretty and charming – little oases of pretty unreasonableness in a vast desert of practical common sense.

Impressions of America

It is a consolation to know, however, that such an artist as Madame Bernhardt has not only worn that yellow, ugly dress, but has been photographed in it.

Impressions of America

Arguments

I dislike arguments of any kind. They are always vulgar, and often convincing.

The Importance of Being Earnest

Art

If something cannot be done to check, or at least modify, our monstrous worship of facts, Art will become sterile, and Beauty will pass away from the land.

The Decay of Lying

Art does not hurt us. The tears that we shed at a play are a type of the exquisite sterile emotions that is the function of Art to awaken. We weep, but we are not wounded. We grieve, but our grief is not bitter.

The Critic as Artist

Beauty

The real tragedy of the poor is that they can afford nothing but self-denial. Beautiful sins, like beautiful things, are the privilege of the rich.

The Picture of Dorian Gray

There is nothing sane about the worship of beauty. It is too splendid to be sane.

The Critic as Artist

Beauty, like Wisdom, loves the lonely worshipper.

The Young King

Brothers

Oh, brothers! I don't care for brothers. My elder brother won't die, and my younger brothers seem never to do anything else.

The Picture of Dorian Gray

Children

Children begin by loving their parents. After a time they judge them. Rarely, if ever, do they forgive them.

A Woman of No Importance

A family is a terrible encumbrance, especially when one is not married.

Vera, or *The Nihilists*

Christ
How else but through a broken heart may Lord Christ enter in?

The Ballad of Reading Gaol

Conversation
I love talking about nothing, father. It is the only thing I know anything about.

An Ideal Husband

I like to do all the talking myself. It saves time and prevents arguments.

The Remarkable Rocket

The simplicity of your character makes you exquisitely incomprehensible to me.

The Importance of Being Earnest

On the Country
Anybody can be good in the country.

The Picture of Dorian Gray

Crime
Murder is always a mistake. One should never do anything that one cannot talk about after dinner.

The Picture of Dorian Gray

Death
One can survive everything nowadays, except death, and live down anything except a good reputation.

A Woman of No Importance

Debt
It is only by not paying one's bills that one can hope to live in the memory of the commercial classes.

Phrases and Philosophies for the Use of the Young

One must have some occupation nowadays. If I hadn't my debts I shouldn't have anything to think about.

A Woman of No Importance

Desperation
She wore far too much rouge last night, and not quite enough clothes. That is always a sign of despair in a woman.

An Ideal Husband

Diaries
I never travel without my diary. One should always have something sensational to read in the train.

The Importance of Being Earnest

Everyone should keep someone else's diary.

Said *in conversation*

Dinner
After a good dinner, one can forgive anybody, even one's own relations.

A Woman of No Importance

Education
The only way to atone for being occasionally a little over-dressed is by being always absolutely over-educated.

Phrases and Philosophies for the Use of the Young

Fortunately in England, at any rate, education produces no effect whatsoever. If it did, it would prove a serious danger to the upper classes, and probably lead to acts of violence in Grosvenor Square.

The Importance of Being Earnest

Education is an admirable thing. But it is well to remember from time to time that nothing that is worth knowing can be taught.

A Few Maxims for the Instruction of the Over-Educated

England and the English
One of those characteristic British faces that once seen are never remembered.

The Picture of Dorian Gray

I can't stand your English house-parties. In England people actually try to be brilliant at breakfast. That is dreadful of them. Only dull people are brilliant at breakfast.

An Ideal Husband

The English public, as a mass, takes no interest in a work of art until it is told that the work in question is immoral.

Letter in defence of *Dorian Gray*

Fascinating people
There are only two kinds of people who are really fascinating – people who know absolutely everything and people who know absolutely nothing.

The Picture of Dorian Gray

Fashion
Fashion is what one wears oneself. What is unfashionable is what other people wear.

An Ideal Husband

Fashion is merely a form of ugliness so unbearable that we are compelled to alter it every six months.

Said *in conversation*

Oscar Wilde

I never saw anybody take so long to dress, and with such little result.

The Importance of Being Earnest

Food and Drink
When I am in trouble, eating is the only thing that consoles me. Indeed, when I am in really great trouble... I refuse everything except food and drink.

The Importance of Being Earnest

For myself, the only immortality I desire is to invent a new sauce.

Vera, or *The Nihilists*

The British cook is a foolish woman – who should be turned for her iniquities into a pillar of salt which she never knows how to use.

Article entitled *Dishes and Dinner*

He never touches water: it goes to his head at once.

Letter

Fools
Remember that the fool in the eyes of the gods and the fool in the eyes of man are very different.

De Profundis

The real fool, such as the gods mock or mar, is he who does not know himself.

De Profundis

Foxhunting
The English country gentleman galloping after a fox – the unspeakable in full pursuit of the uneatable.

A Woman of No Importance

Friendship
I shall never make a new friend in my life, though perhaps a few after I die.

Said *in conversation*

On God
God would grow weary if I told my sins.

The Duchess of Padua

God's house is the only house where sinners are made welcome.

A Woman of No Importance

God used poverty often as a means of bringing people to Him, and used riches never, or but rarely.

Letter *to Robert Ross*

On Good friends
She is without one good quality, she lacks the finest spark of decency and is quite the wickedest woman in London. I haven't a word to say in her favour… and she is one of my greatest friends.

Said *in conversation*

Gossip and Scandal
I don't at all like knowing what people say of me behind my back. It makes one far too conceited.

An Ideal Husband

I love scandals about other people, but scandals about myself don't interest me. They have not got the charm of novelty.

The Picture of Dorian Gray

Everything you have said today seems to me excessively immoral. It has been most interesting, listening to you.

A Woman of No Importance

It is perfectly monstrous the way people go about nowadays saying things against one behind one's back that are absolutely and entirely true.

The Picture of Dorian Gray

Hair
The youth of the present day are quite monstrous. They have absolutely no respect for dyed hair.

Lady Windermere's Fan

Health
Why don't you ask me how I am? I like people to ask me how I am. It shows a widespread interest in my health.

Lady Windermere's Fan

On having a heart
I thought I had no heart. I find I have, and a heart doesn't suit me, Windermere. Somehow it doesn't go with modern dress. It makes one look old and it spoils one's career at critical moments.

Lady Windermere's Fan

House of Commons
The House of Commons really does very little harm. You can't make people good by Act of Parliament.

A Woman of No Importance

There is hardly a single person in the House of Commons worth painting; though many of them would be better for a little whitewashing.

The Picture of Dorian Gray

On being humble
Praise makes me humble, but when I am abused I know I have touched the stars.

Said *in conversation*

Ignorance
Ignorance is like a delicate exotic fruit; touch it and the bloom is gone.

The Importance of Being Earnest

On being asked if he was ill:
No, not ill, but very weary. The fact is I picked a primrose in the wood yesterday, and it was so ill that I have been sitting up with it all night.

Said *in conversation*

On imprisonment
The most terrible thing about it [imprisonment] is not that it breaks one's heart – hearts are made to be broken – but that it turns one's heart to stone.

De Profundis

I have the horror of death with the still greater horror of living.

Letter *to Robert Ross*

To those who are in prison, tears are part of every day's experience. A day in prison on which one does not weep is a day on which one's heart is hard, not a day on which one's heart is happy.

De Profundis

Impartiality
It is only about things that do not interest me that one can give a really unbiased opinion, which is no doubt the reason why an unbiased opinion is always absolutely valueless.

The Critic as Artist

Income
It is better to have a permanent income than to be fascinating.

A Model Millionaire

On Henry James
Mr Henry James writes fiction as if it were a painful duty.

The Decay of Lying

On Journalists
In the old days men had the rack. Now they have the Press.

The Soul of Man Under Socialism

With regard to modern journalists, they always apologise to one in private for what they have written against one in public.

The Soul of Man Under Socialism

Spies are of no use nowadays. Their profession is over. The newspapers do their work instead.

An Ideal Husband

Kindness
Prisoners are, as a class, extremely kind and sympathetic to each other. Suffering and the community of suffering make people kind. It is not the prisoners who need reformation. It is the prisons.

Letter *to* 'Daily Chronicle'

The only really humanising influence in prison is the influence of the prisoners.

De Profundis

What is a kiss?
A kiss may ruin a human life.

A Woman of No Importance

On Letter-writing
How could I have written to you during the last three months considering that I have been in bed since last Monday?

Letter *to Robert Ross*

What is life?
The world is a stage, but the play is badly cast.

Lord Arthur Savile's Crime

Life cheats us with shadows, life a puppet-master. We ask it for pleasure. It gives it to us, with bitterness and disappointment in its train.

The Critic as Artist

We are all in the gutter but some of us are looking at the stars.

Lady Windermere's Fan

For when one looks back upon the life that was so vivid in its emotional intensity, and filled with such fervent moments of ecstasy and joy, it all seems to be a dream and an illusion.

The Critic as Artist

The secret of life is to appreciate the pleasure of being terribly, terribly deceived.

A Woman of No Importance

The secret of life is to resist temptation.

A Woman of No Importance

Listening
One should never listen. To listen is a sign of indifference to one's hearers.

A Few Maxims for the Instruction of the Over-Educated

I hate people who talk about themselves, as you do, when one wants to talk about oneself, as I do.

The Remarkable Rocket

Literature
If one cannot enjoy reading a book over and over again, there is no use reading it at all.

The Decay of Lying

The books that the world calls immoral books are books that show the world its own shame.

The Picture of Dorian Gray

On Love
Love can read the writing on the remotest star.

De Profundis

Love does not traffic in a marketplace, nor use a huckster's scales. Its joy, like the joy of the intellect, is to feel oneself alive. The aim of Love is to love: no more and no less. There is no prison in any world into which Love cannot force an entrance.

De Profundis

Only love can keep anyone alive.

A Woman of No Importance

All love is terrible. All love is tragedy.

A Woman of No Importance

All lives, save loveless lives, true Love should pardon.
A man's love is like that. It is wider, larger, more human
than a woman's.

An Ideal Husband

Yet each man kills the thing he loves.

The Ballad of Reading Gaol

Matrimony
I was in hopes he would have married Lady Kelso. But
I believe he said her family was too large. Or was it her
feet? I forget which.

A Woman of No Importance

You don't seem to realise, that in married life three is
company and two is none.

The Importance of Being Earnest

Loveless marriages are horrible. But there is one thing worse than an absolutely loveless marriage. A marriage in which there is love, but on one side only; faith, but on one side only; devotion, but on one side only, and in which of the two hearts one is sure to be broken.

An Ideal Husband

Marriage is hardly a thing that one can do now and then – except in America.

The Picture of Dorian Gray

Men
The General was essentially a man of peace, except in his domestic life.

The Importance of Being Earnest

When a man is old enough to do wrong he should be old enough to do right also.

A Woman of No Importance

Every man nowadays has his disciples, and it is always Judas who writes the biography.

The Critic as Artist

Oscar Wilde

He was eccentric, I admit. But only in later years. And that was the result of the Indian climate, and marriage, and indigestion, and other things of that kind.

The Importance of Being Earnest

On Mussels
My doctor has been trying to cure me with arsenic and strychnine but without much success as I became poisoned through mussels. So you see what an exacting and tragic life I have been leading. Poisoning by mussels is very painful and when one has one's bath one looks like a leopard. Pray never eat mussels.

Letter *to Robert Ross*

Needlework
She ultimately was so broken-hearted that she went into a convent, or on to the operatic stage, I forget which. No; I think it was decorative art-needlework she took up.

An Ideal Husband

Niagara Falls
Niagara Falls is simply a vast unnecessary amount of water going the wrong way and then falling over unnecessary rocks.

Said *in conversation*

Nobody
Nobody, even in the provinces, should ever be allowed to ask an intelligent question about pure mathematics across a dinner table.

The Art of Conversation

Oscar on Oscar
It is sad. One half of the world does not believe in God and the other half does not believe in me.

Said *in conversation*

I never put off until tomorrow what I can possibly do – the day after.

Said *in conversation*

I am always thinking about myself, and I expect everybody else to do the same.

The Remarkable Rocket

If life be, as it surely is, a problem to me, I am no less a problem to life.

De Profundis

I can resist everything except temptation.

Lady Windermere's Fan

Opinion
Whistler is indeed one of the very greatest masters of painting in my opinion. And may I add that in this opinion Mr Whistler himself entirely concurs.

Mr Whistler's Ten O'Clock

Optimism
People who count their chickens before they are hatched, act very wisely, because chickens run about so absurdly that it is impossible to count them accurately.

Letter

Outdoor games
I am afraid I play no outdoor games at all. Except dominoes. I have sometimes played dominoes outside French cafés.

Said *in conversation*

Parents

To lose one parent, Mr Worthing, may be regarded as a misfortune; to lose both looks like carelessness.

The Importance of Being Earnest

On Philanthropists

Philanthropy is the refuge of people who wish to annoy their fellow creatures.

An Ideal Husband

On plays

I never write plays for anyone. I write plays to amuse myself. After, if people want to act in them, I sometimes allow them to do so.

Said *in conversation*

My dear Alex, it was charming, quite charming. And, do you know, from time to time I was reminded of a play I once wrote myself called *The Importance of Being Earnest*.

Said *in conversation, to George Alexander, Theatre Manager on* The Importance of Being Earnest

Poverty

I am never in during the afternoon, except when I am confined to the house by a sharp attack of penury.

Letter

Nowadays we are all of us so hard up that the only pleasant things to pay are compliments. They're the only things we *can* pay.

Lady Windermere's Fan

There is only one class in the community that thinks more about money than the rich, and that is the poor. The poor can think of nothing else.

The Soul of Man under Socialism

Public

I am very fond of the public, and, personally, I always patronise the public very much.

Said *in conversation*

They love me very much – simple loyal people; give them a new saint, it costs nothing.

Vera or *The Nihilists*

Queen Victoria
Sir, if this is the way Queen Victoria treats her convicts she doesn't deserve to have any.

Said *in conversation*

The Queen is not a subject.

Said *in conversation on being asked to discuss the Queen as a subject.*

Questions
Questions are never indiscreet. Answers sometimes are.

An Ideal Husband

I have nothing to declare but my genius.

Said *in conversation, on being questioned by Customs in New York*

Relations
I can't help detesting my relations. I suppose it comes from the fact that none of us can stand other people having the same faults as ourselves.

The Picture of Dorian Gray

I love hearing my relations abused. It is the only thing that makes me put up with them at all.

The Importance of Being Earnest

Relations never lend one any money and won't give one credit, even for genius. They are a sort of aggravated form of the public.

The Importance of Being Earnest

Religion
It is very difficult to keep awake, especially in church.

The Canterville Ghost

Prayer must never be answered: if it is, it ceases to be prayer and becomes correspondence.

Said *in conversation*

A sermon is but a sorry sauce, when you have nothing to eat it with.

The Duchess of Padua

When I think about religion at all, I feel as if I would like to found an order for those who *cannot* believe.

De Profundis

Reputations
A good reputation is one of the many annoyances to which I have never been subjected.

A Woman of No Importance

Revelations
The Book of Life begins with a man and woman in a garden. It ends with Revelations.

A Woman of No Importance

Romance
To love oneself is the beginning of a lifelong romance.

An Ideal Husband

One should always be in love. That is the reason one should never marry.

A Woman of No Importance

Whatever my life may have been ethically, it has always been *romantic*.

Letter

Schooldays
I have forgotten about my schooldays. I have a vague impression that they were detestable.

An Ideal Husband

Selfishness
Selfishness is not living as one wishes to live, it is asking others to live as one wishes to live.

The Soul of Man under Socialism

Sin
As a wicked man I am a complete failure. Why, there are lots of people who say I have never really done anything wrong in the whole course of my life. Of course they only say it behind my back.

Lady Windermere's Fan

If your sins find you out, why worry! It is when they find you *in*, that trouble begins.

Said *in conversation*

I hope you have not been leading a double life, pretending to be wicked and being really good all the time, that would be hypocrisy.

The Importance of Being Earnest

The only difference between the saint and the sinner is that every saint has a past, and every sinner has a future.

A Woman of No Importance

Society
Other people are quite dreadful. The only possible society is oneself.

An Ideal Husband

Success
Anybody can sympathise with the sufferings of a friend, but it requires a very fine nature – it requires, in fact, the nature of a true Individualist – to sympathise with a friend's success.

The Soul of Man under Socialism

Ties
A well-tied tie is the first serious step in life.

A Woman of No Importance

Truth
If one tells the truth, one is sure, sooner or later, to be found out.

Phrases and Philosophies for the Use of the Young

The truth isn't quite the sort of thing that one tells to a nice, sweet, refined girl.

The Importance of Being Earnest

The truth is rarely pure, and never simple.

The Importance of Being Earnest

The truth about the life of a man is not what he does, but the legend which he creates around himself.

Said *in conversation*

Typewriters
The typewriting machine, when played with expression is no more annoying than the piano when played by a sister or near relation.

Letter *to Robert Ross*

Unpunctuality
Punctuality is the thief of time – I am not punctual myself, but I do like punctuality in others.

Said *in conversation*

I am due at the Athenaeum [club]. It is the hour when we sleep there.

The Picture of Dorian Gray

Vanity
Nothing makes one so vain as being told that one is a sinner.

The Picture of Dorian Gray

Vice
He hasn't a single redeeming vice.

Said *in conversation*

On Virtues

You flatter her. She has her virtues as most women have, but beauty is a gem she may not wear.

A Florentine Tragedy

Don't be led astray into the paths of virtue.

Lady Windermere's Fan

Visitors

The most comfortable chair is the one I use myself when I have visitors.

An Ideal Husband

Oh, I'm so glad that you have come. There are a hundred things I want not to say to you.

Said *in conversation*

Wallpaper

My wallpaper and I are fighting a duel to the death. One or the other of us has to go.

Said *in conversation*

Oscar Wilde

War

As long as war is regarded as wicked, it will always have its fascination. When it is looked upon as vulgar, it will cease to be popular.

The Critic as Artist

Wealth

What this century worships is wealth. The God of this century is wealth. To succeed one must have wealth. At all costs one must have wealth.

An Ideal Husband

Weather

Whenever people talk to me about the weather, I always feel certain that they mean something else.

The Importance of Being Earnest

Women and Wives

Because the husband is vile – should the wife be vile also?

Lady Windermere's Fan

Her capacity for family affection is extraordinary. When her third husband died, her hair turned quite gold from grief.

The Picture of Dorian Gray

It is only the very ugly or very beautiful women who ever hide their faces.

The Duchess of Padua

What are called good women may have terrible things in them, mad moods of recklessness, assertion, jealousy, sin. Bad women, as they are termed, may have in them sorrow, repentance, pity, sacrifice.

Lady Windermere's Fan

On Work
Work is simply the refuge of people who have nothing whatever to do.

The Remarkable Rocket

Work is the curse of the drinking classes.

Lady Windermere's Fan

It is awfully hard work doing nothing. However, I don't mind hard work where there is no definite object of any kind.

The Importance of Being Earnest

Man is made for something better than disturbing dirt. All work of that kind should be done by machine.

The Soul of Man

Writing
Everything I write is extraordinary. I do not pose as being ordinary, great heavens!

Said *in reply to Sir Edward Carson, on being cross-examined*

I write because it gives me the greatest possible artistic pleasure to write. If my work pleases the few I am gratified. As for the mob, I have no desire to be a popular novelist. It is far too easy.

Letter *in defence of* Dorian Gray

I wrote when I did not know life; now that I do know the meaning of life, I have no more to write. Life cannot be written; life can only be lived.

Said in conversation

The 'X' Factor
I am sick of women who love me. Women who hate me are much more interesting.

The Picture of Dorian Gray

Youth
In America the young are always ready to give those who are older than themselves the full benefits of their inexperience.

The American Invasion

The old believe everything; the middle-aged suspect everything; the young know everything.

Phrases and Philosophies for the Use of the Young

To get back my youth I would do anything in the world, except take exercise, get up early, or be respectable.

The Picture of Dorian Gray

There is nothing like youth. The middle-aged are mortgaged to Life. The old are in Life's lumber room. But youth is the Lord of Life.

A Woman of No Importance

And at the end?
As soon as people are old enough to know better, they don't know anything at all.

Lady Windermere's Fan

I don't regret for a single moment having lived for pleasure. I did it to the full, as one should do everything that one does to the full. There was no pleasure I did not experience.

De Profundis

Acknowledgements

The publisher wishes to thank the following for permission to reproduce work in copyright:

© istockphoto.com / DNY59 (p4)
© istockphoto.com. Photograph by Hulton Archive/ Getty images (pp6, 10, 14, 16, 25, 30, 36, 40 and 44)
© istockphoto.com. Photograph by Picture Post/ Getty images (p18)
© istockphoto.com. Photograph by Rischgitz/ Getty images (p26 and 34)
© Library of Congress. Prints and Photographs Division (pp47, 50, 60, 74 and 88)

Faber and Faber Ltd for "In Memory of W.B. Yeats" by W.H. Auden; Maurice Craig for "Ballad To A Traditional Refrain"; Blackstaff Press for "Ulster Names" by John Hewitt (from *The Collected Poems of John Hewitt,* edited by Frank Ormsby); the Trustees of the Estate of Patrick Kavanagh, c/o Peter Fallon, Literary Agent, Loughcrew, Oldcastle, Co. Meath, Ireland, for "Stony Grey Soil" by Patrick Kavanagh; Hugh Leonard for the excerpts from *Home Before Night* and *Da;* HarperCollins Publishers Ltd for *The Screwtape Letters* by C.S. Lewis; Michael Williams, Executor of the Estate of the late Dr Hilton Edwards, for the quotation by Micheál mac Liammóir; Paddy MacManus for "Praise God For Ireland" by Francis McManus; Faber and Faber Ltd for "Western Landscape" by Louis MacNeice; Conor Cruise

O'Brien for his quotation; HarperCollins Publishers Ltd for quotations from *At Swim-Two-Birds* and *The Third Policeman* by Flann O'Brien; Eileen O'Casey and Macmillan London Ltd for the quotations by Sean O'Casey; the Society of Authors on behalf of the Bernard Shaw Estate for the quotation from *Immaturity;* the Curtis Brown Group Ltd, London, for the quotation from *Some Experiences of an Irish RM* by Somerville and Ross; Felicitas Corrigan for "I Shall Not Go To Heaven" by Helen Waddell. Appletree Press for quotations from *The Quiet Man and Other Stories* by Maurice Walsh; *The Collegians* by Gerald Griffin; *Ormond* by Maria Edgeworth and *Lord Kilgobbin* by Charles Lever.

While every effort has been made to contact copyright holders, the publisher would welcome information on any oversight which may have occurred.